HOW TO SELECT A GURU

HOW TO SELECT A GURU

Ramamurti S. Mishra

PILGRIMS PUBLISHING
Varanasi•Kathmandu

HOW TO SELECT A GURU

By Ramamurti S Mishra

Published by
PILGRIMS PUBLISHING

An imprint of
PILGRIMS BOOK HOUSE
B 27/98 A-8, Nawabganj Road
Durga Kund
Varanasi, India 221010
Tel: 91-542-314060, 312496
Fax: 91-542-314059
E-mail: pilgrims@satyam.net.in

Distributed in India by
BOOK FAITH INDIA
414-416 Express Tower
Azadpur Commercial Complex
New Delhi-110033, India
Tel: 91-11-713-2459
Fax: 91-11-724-9674
E-mail: pilgrim@del2.vsnl.net.in

Distributed in Nepal by
PILGRIMS BOOK HOUSE
P.O Box 3872
Kathmandu, Nepal
Tel: 977-1-424942
Fax: 977-1-424943
E-mail: pilgrims@wlink.com.np

First published in New York by
ICSA Press

ISBN 81-7769-029-9

Edited by C.N. Burchett
Layout by Hom KC
Cover design by Dr. Sasya

Printed in India

Contents

Introduction to the New Edition

Yoga, if practiced properly and with the guidance of an experienced teacher, will always lead one to the heights of spiritual exhilaration and ecstasy. It is all so easy to just start and get lost in a maze of damaging experiences which later cause irreparable damage or produce such painful and hateful experiences that one may even teeter on the borders of insanity.

This short booklet explains quite clearly how one should choose a teacher (Guru) and the ways in which to know his qualities. It also goes on to tell us how to recognise whether the experiences we may have are taking us in the right directions or not. To qualify this the author has given us several case histories to show the need for a proper teacher and proper involvement in the studies of yoga and meditation.

How to Select
a
GURU

He who is in search of a guru should first seek the guru within himself. If he seeks the guru outside without seeking the guru within himself, then he is consciously and unconsciously stupefying himself.

He who has no faith and no confidence in his own inner guru, and is trying to have faith and confidence in his outer guru, such a person may enjoy his illusions for a while, but ultimately he is forced to be disillusioned. It is sure that one cannot live without a guru, but it is equally sure that the search of a guru begins first within, then in the outer guru, then in God. Ultimately, the Soul of the individual and that of the external guru and God become one.

'Guru' consists of two syllables: 'Gu' and 'Ru'; 'Gu' means darkness, and 'Ru' remover. He who removes the darkness from our understanding is the real guru, and such a guru and his office are always open in our hearts. He is forever young and eternal, and his teachings are direct without language. They are in the language of feeling and revealing, but if one cannot contact directly this inner guru, then one must search for the outer guru.

The outer guru is he who guides the true seeker into this inner journey for the intimate contact with the inner guru. That which is beyond this light and darkness is the true Light.

To have contact with this true light we need first-hand knowledge of the inner journey. The process which is guiding us into our inner journey is called initiation

Initiation

Meeting with such a person who has experienced the intimate contact with this true light, and who radiates this light of truth and harmony to his environment and to the Cosmos, is an essential part in our growth toward inner experience.

God has two forms: the absolute and the Revealed. The absolute form of God is called NIRGUNA, or impersonal aspect of God; but the manifestation of the Absolute God in the human heart is called personal or SAGUNA aspect.

From a practical point of view, he who understands mentally this Absolute aspect of God is an illumined person psychologically, but he is not enlightened spiritually.

He who knows how to transform the Absolute into his personal life is an Enlightened One, and this transformation of Absolute into one's personal activities is called the SAGUNA aspect of God.

He who facilitates the transaction of transformation of SAGUNA to NIRGUNA and NIRGUNA to SAGUNA is the real guru. Such a guru is radiating a finer vibration of being, which purifies the ethereal ocean and rejuvenates those around him.

The external form of guru is like the central station of an airport, the inner form of guru is like catching an airplane, and the spiritual form of guru is like the traveller himself enjoying the journey. The physical form of guru helps physically and the psychological form of guru helps psychologically; but both these forms of guru, as well as the disciple and the world are constantly changing; therefore, they are not reliable.

The true form of guru, disciple, and the world is essentially the Spirit, which cannot be described to anybody except those who practice meditation day and night. This Spiritual aspect is like the eating of the dumb person, who enjoys eating, and expresses a happiness of eating through his feeling, but he has no tongue to describe it. He who is trying hard to experience his inner guru, will easily find an outer guru also to help him in his inner journey.

The guru's guidance verbally helps in the understanding of our mental and physical functions, manifestations, and problems, so that we may begin on the path of self inquiry in all ways-directly and indirectly- positively and negatively. The duty of the guru is to pass the information, and the duty of the disciple is to practice and to transform the information into his blood.

The guru cannot give someone his own enlightenment. Satya Sai Baba could not produce another spiritual magician or an enlightened person like himself, although he is surrounded by thousands and thousands of seekers. Truth cannot be conveyed through language; each individual has to experience this Truth in his heart because the experience of others cannot be his own experience. The guru stands as a light to direct the way within and without, and those who have the eyes of wisdom see and feel that light.

There are many teachers in the world, and there are also a few teachers who understand the ultimate nature of reality; also there are many refined institutions where wonderful training is given to disciples to experience the inner truth but, believe it or not, one gets only as much understanding as one deserves. Everybody understands reality according to his own ability and capacity, rather than the Ultimate Reality itself; therefore, your guru can be only he who understands you, and whom you understand. God is present everywhere, and he is worshipped by practically all; but everyone understands God not as God is, but according to his own ability and capacity; so everybody has a different idea about God and guru and the world.

Regarding the subject matter of reality, not only is everyone different from one another, but also the same person is different from moment to moment. As one's experience grows higher and higher, so one's consciousness expands into a higher and higher aspect or plane of reality.

Now you tell me how to answer 'What is guru, and who is guru?' God helps those who help themselves, and vice versa, God does not help those who do not help themselves. Likewise, those who already have the tendency toward a natural inner journey and inner experience, are progressively growing, they understand all aspects of the guru.

The guru is the greatest catalyst in our journey, and he is the moving image of God; he is experienced by us according to our needs, desires, and understanding.

Ultimately, inner guru, outer guru and God submerge into the reality which is called One-without-a-second. A guru does not teach anybody to depend on him, nor does he pretend to be the guru of anybody. Those who declare themselves to be a guru, and those who pretend to be the guru-definitely they are not.

The guru is the moving image of God; therefore, he radiates not individuality, but the Universal aspect of Truth.

A guru also has anxieties, frustrations, depressions, and worries, but all these feelings in him are divine and impersonal. His anxiety is to see others in God consciousness, his depression from the path of truth, his frustrations are for those students who are not getting any experience of bliss. He has worries in removing the difficulty of others and making them full of bliss. Accordingly, his anger is like a thunderbolt; however, it is not for selfish purposes, but to enlighten students. In short, the guru has all those habits which we have, but in him they are all impersonal and divine, while in others they are human and personal ultimately leading to animal passions.

So here lies the difficulty to judge a guru. A guru may beat you to the point of your final breath, but yet you will experience enlightenment in that! A skillful and powerful enemy can offer you a sweet and tasty meal, but it may contain poison in it; therefore, can you judge a man only by his sweet action or bitter action?

By action we cannot judge or select a guru, that is to say we cannot judge a guru positively, but negatively. He who has no injurious thoughts to anybody physically, mentally, or vocally; he who has no business mind, he who is not using guruship as an economic cult, he who has no nature of exploiting others, he who does not hate anybody under any condition; such a person who is free from these qualities is a guru.

Positively he can be described as a guru if he is integrally related to the total Universe. He who has natural compassion, friendship, fellowship, and kindness to all beings, he who loves All unconditionally and yet remains beyond all, is a true guru. This guru is the natural and crystal-clear picture of God.

Until we have met spontaneously with such a teacher within us, to be constantly on the lookout and search for a guru outside becomes superfluous; it is wrong because in this constant searching and looking we forget the experience of our inner awareness, which in constant and continuous self analysis, leading to the awareness of cosmic consciousness, we realize that every person and situation we meet within life can become our guru.

Nature is the ultimate teacher, and it has only one goal for all beings, especially all human beings: to bring them from the field of multiplicity into the realm of unity. With this outlook one can see the misdirectedness of those who claim that 'The guru' they have met with, is the one and only world enlightened one, and by no other teacher can one attain such grace. In the same vein, those 'gurus' who claim that they are the avatar of the age, they definitely create a storm of confusion with their claims.

Are there degrees in a guru? Some are claimed to have direct contact with god, and nobody will see god without their intervention. Some religions have similar claims, so there is a natural inquiry:

"Are there grades of gurus?"

"My guru is greater than your guru"

or

"My guru knows something which your guru does not know."

or

"My guru remains one half of the day silent and eats only raw food."

or

"My guru has more buildings than your guru."

Some gurus have twenty sports cars, a helicopter, an airplane, and thirty-three Rolls Royces.

Who gives this name of guru to them?

They design the name of 'guru' by their own pen, and some have wonderful business agencies; their programs are very attractive; and well advertised-but the question is: "can external prosperity be the sign of a perfect guru?"

Some even have a monopoly on the various names of meditation, have trade-marks on a particular style of meditation, and sell mantras at a fixed fee. Where will you fit them? I am not telling you who they are, I am asking you: What do you think about this matter? In this confused situation can anybody have courage to tell truly, honestly, and openly "Who is the guru?"

The true guru is he who removes the power of competition and jealousy from your heart, and makes your heart able to love not only all gurus of the world, but all creatures of the world, not only all fellows of the present, but also fellows of the past and future.

When there 'is union with a guru. All selfishness, evil tendencies, chaos, disharmony, ignorance, egoism, misunderstanding, greed, lust, and hatred disappear and there is an uninterrupted flow of love, understanding, togetherness, selfless service, gratefulness and compassion.

In this eternal flow of cosmic energy, all multiplicity channels itself into one main flow a union with god force!

This one-without-a-second is called guru.

We can say that the real guru is like a mirror, evaluating anything brought in the presence of his light. A true guru is he through whom you can experience your self, the total humanity, all incarnations of God, and all phases of the universe.

Man minus selfishness is God, and God plus selfishness is man.

There are many things to be said regarding this matter, and many books have been written on this subject; but here I am writing just a few lines limited in number, and I hope these lines will give you total understanding of the fact. Then you can write your own book, if you have time.

What is True Shakti Pat *Versus* Pseudo Shakti Pat?

SHAKTIPAT

In the experience of the operation of Cosmic energy man is transformed into immanent and transcendental form of the self and he enjoys the omnipresence, omnipotence, and omniscience of his true self. In devotional language, he is the true Son of God.

But the relation of son and father with God is not a relative experience, but it is supratranscendental and indescribable by the mind. "I and my father are one."

"The research of Kundalini awakening will bring to light three cardinal issues about which the world is at present completely in the dark.

The first is the discovery that the reproductive system also acts as the evolutionary mechanism. The second is that the religious impulse is based on inherent evolutionary tendencies in the psyche. And the third is that there is a predetermined target for the irresistibly drawn towards it."

"Science has entirely ignored the spiritual side of man and devoted all its attention to the physical and organic fields." "Lust for power and status is the basic cause for the present disorder in society. Simple living and high thinking should be the motto of life."

Margaret Coble

"Only the Force of our God-self is true Illumination, and that requires correct understanding. Otherwise Shakti remains a force of fascination and ignorance."

"The awakening of Kundalini (the divine power that lies dormant in every human being at the base of spinal chord in the form of a coiled serpent) through yoga or other subtle disciplines produces a scientifically measurable biochemical essence that is responsible for the phenomenon of genius as well as for the process of evolution in man."

"This evolution is towards a transcendental state of consciousness which has characterized the Buddha, Christ, Vyasa; Shankaracharya and all great luminaries of mankind."

"By empirical research it has to be shown that this condition of consciousness is the ultimate target of human evolution."

"In all human beings there is a powerful reservoir of psychic energy which when roused to activity in the state of kundalini can lead

16

to transcendental states of consciousness, genius and supernatural psychic powers. In the state of kundalini awakening, the reproductive system recoils on itself and transfers energy to the brain. We can learn to activate kundalini only through devoted meditation and yogic exercises, not by manipulation of the mind or artificially created changes. Everyone is passing through the process of evolution to a higher state of consciousness".

Gopi Krishna

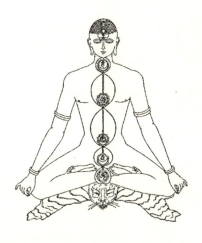

The seven chakras (subtle centers of energy) along the susumna (central nervous system) are listed below with their related sounds.

MULADHARA (मूलाधार)
At the base of the spine near the reproductive organs. The sound for this Chakra is LAM (लँ)

SVADHISTHANA (स्वाधिष्ठान)
A little above the muladhara chakra; the sound for this chakra is VAM (वँ)

MANIPURA (मणिपुर)
In the center of the stomach: the sound for this chakra is RAM (रँ)

ANAHATA (अनाहत)
In the heart; the sound for this chakra is YAM (यँ)

VISHUDDHA (विशुद्ध)
In the throat; the sound is HAM (हँ)

AJNA (आज्ञा)
Center of forehead sometimes referred to as the 'third eye' the sound for this chakra is OM (ॐ)

SAHASRARA (सहस्रार) ... in the Cerebral Cortex; this Chakra vibrates with all the sounds.

The words 'Coiled Energy'. Refer to the KUNDALINI SHAKTI (कुण्डलिनी शक्ति), the energy manifested in the human body, specially through the channel of Susumna (सुषुम्णा), the central nervous system.

What is Shakti Pat?

We are hearing a lot of news and rumors about the awakening of kundalini shakti and shakti pat, and the sudden awakening of cosmic consciousness, and receiving constant letters inquiring about it.

What is shakti pat, and what is the rising of kundalini power? Every being is a miniature micro-cosmic universe. Man is micro-cosmic. They are one and the same in every moment of time and space, but seemingly there is a dichotomy between these two.

Within the individual total Cosmic forces are coiled up (latent) and they are sleeping potentially. When the individual Karmas are dwindling ... then this sleeping coiled potentiality begins to sprout. This blossoming of potentially sleeping micro-cosmic force is called the rising of kundalini and the experience of this rising begins with shakti pat.

There are innumerable ways of this force to rise. Naturally, in every human being there is the central nervous system which has bi-way path systems from the base of the spine to the top of the head. Forces are moving constantly carrying on sensations and motions, and this bi-way depends on the central nervous system and on the peripheral nervous system, including both the voluntary and involuntary systems. These bi-way motions in the central nervous system constantly and continuously operate in every being, although they are not felt by everyone. Because of preoccupied mind and because of Karmas, man has no way to experience them.

But, when up to an extent Karmas are dwindled and human intelligence becomes sharp, keen, serious and sincere about the meaning and purpose of life on this earth, then one begins to experience these forces as the opening of a screw in the Muladhara Chakra (base of spine) and rising to the crown of the head, Sahasrara Chakra, with innumerable phenomena.

कुण्डलिन्यां समुद्भूता गायत्री प्राणधारिणी ।
प्राणविद्या महाविद्या यस्तां वेत्ति स वेदवित् ॥

**Originating within the Kundalini is the
great Goddess Gayatri, sustainer of
Prana, the life force. She herself is the
Knowledge of Life, the Great Science;
he who knows her, truly knows the
meaning of all scriptures.**

For example, some experience hot and cold sensation, with ordinary heat and cold up to tremendous and stupendous heat and cold, and ultimately they feel transformation of this energy into various lights and colors. Some are even frightened, while others experience a euphoria pervading the whole being. Sudden surges of energy like electrical charges shake the whole spine, and ultimately and gradually these energy waves become a steady hot and cold current, flowing from the base of the spine to the top of the head. Brilliant colors, especially having blue pearls radiating with blue and blue-green whitish color, begin to burst with happiness and bliss. Various other uncontrollable phenomena come, like jerking in the body, a desire to shout, chant, dance, howl, and so on and so forth.

In brief, it is the blossoming of individual force into the cosmic force or transformation of the individual spirit into the universal spirit. But this is not the only way of rising of kundalini and the experience of shakti pat. There are innumerable other higher ways than this way such as automatic opening of Vedas (the holy scriptures of India), automatic and spontaneous knowledge of the Sanskrit language (the divine language), in which the vedas are written. A man who has never known the Vedas or the Sanskrit language begins to speak Sanskrit and begins to speak through direct mantras of the Vedas. Some even begin to feel the breathing in and of the vibration of all holy scriptures through every hair particle, while others begin to experience pulsation of all stars through every cell of their body. There are many other manifestations, which to describe would take the form of a large book, and therefore are beyond the scope of this article.

In this awakening neither does anybody enter inside the body nor does anybody go outside; it is just the breathing of the true Spirit, which you can call God. As there are various phenomena of shakti pat, so there are many ways of shakti pat. Chiefly they can be summarized in two classes:

1. Sudden and instant awakening of Cosmic Consciousness,
2. Gradual awakening of Cosmic Consciousness.

The gradual awakening is natural and does not present any hallucinative and psychopathological phenomena. But the sudden and instant awakening presents a problem.

Some even have been reported to remain a long time in a state very similar to insanity, and some being under psychiatric treatment also. It took a long time to recognize that their manifestations were not psychiatric but divine in nature.

By the combination of the first and second, a third variety is reported in the scriptures.

This means, on and off, instant and sudden awakening of various planes of Cosmic Consciousness, and between these awakenings a gradual process of awakening continues. The following enlightened persons are an example of this third variety:

Shri Jagannath Mishra, Nimai Mishra (Chaitanya Mahaprabhu), the original founder of Krishna consciousness in the 15th century.

Shri Paramahansa Rama Krishna – the world renowned teacher and guru of Shri Swami Vivekananda – founder of Ramakrishna Centers.

Shri Krishnamurti – whose Kundalini began to awaken in the Ojai valley in California. He experienced tremendous pain in his back and head. A current was running with hot and cold sensations starting at the top of his head, reaching to the point of feeling 'two serpents' moving up the spinal column and meeting together between the two eyes, in the center of his head. These manifestations lasted several years giving him difficulties mostly in the nose and in the back of the head until all of a sudden he forgot everything and lost complete memory. From that day on he became a different person. He felt in himself that he was Buddha, that he was Christ, that he was Krishna and Lord Maitreya. Many things came; you can read of this process in Mary Lutyen's book – "The Years of Awakening – Krishnamurti".

The following enlightened persons are an example of the first variety:

Bhagavan Shri Ramana Maharshi – had instant awakening of Kundalini. Without warning and while in a good state of health he suddenly felt strongly that he was going to die.

This shock turned him inward and instead of giving in to fear and phobia he began to ask himself, "Now death has come, what does it mean? What is it that is dying? This body will be carried to the burning ground and reduced to ashes. But with the death of this body am I dead? The body is dead." At this moment he experienced that he was not the body, but the spirit that transcends all bodies, and he was awakened from that moment on. All of the holy scriptures were revealed to him. He could read and interpret in many languages including Sanskrit, which he had not known before. He became the greatest person in a moment.

The great poet Kalidas, the Shakespeare of India, is reported to have had instant shakti pat. He fell down on a piece of stone crying the name of the cosmic mother for help — instead of having an accident he began to speak divine language, and the vedas began to vibrate in his breathing and thoughts. He became the greatest scholar of the Sanskrit language in a moment. A very similar incident is reported about Edgar Cayce in the US

Shri Gopi Krishna's story is world famous and I do not need to project much light about that. His book is available by the name of "Awakening of Kundalini". I highly recommend this book for readers on this topic. Shri Gopi Krishna also passed through phenomena of tremendous and stupendous pain, misery and suffering, but ultimately he obtained perfection on his path. His books will tell the reader the story of his life, written by him.

Most other enlightened persons are the example of gradual and natural awakening of cosmic consciousness.

If careful study is done on this subject, especially careful study of the books of Gopi Krishna, M.P. Pandit from the Aurobindo Ashram in Pondicherri, India, and Sir John Woodroffe, then a scientific system can be established regarding this path; and I am sure many seekers of truth can be saved from the serious consequences of the instant shakti pat.

Every year thousands and thousands of people are railroaded for admission into mental institutes, and I am sure if not all of them, most of them can be saved and ultimately can be brought to the point of genuine awakening of cosmic consciousness.

We have two anarchies going on in our society. The first is the anarchy of pseudo-spiritual teachers about sakti pat, who are trying to imitate the outer manifestations and trying to create artificial phenomena such as howling, shouting, jumping, chattering of teeth, and shrieking etc.

No doubt these phenomena may come with genuine awakening also, but they should not be confused with phenomena artificially produced in a seeker in order to obtain the panorama of cosmic consciousness.

How can we know the genuine manifestation of shakti pat from the artificially induced shakti pat? I will advise all friends to know the difference between natural sleep and the sleep artificially produced by drugs. Artificially produced sleep by means of drugs may lead to degeneration of the nervous system and finally to insanity. Likewise artificially induced shakti pat is a dangerous way of awakening kundalini shakti.

I have found many institutions and many teachers, also many seekers, interested in inducing artificial Shakti pat. In the beginning they seem to work very well, but ultimately I found them very neurotic, psychotic and cruel, and they can even act with absolute insanity towards those who are not 'with' them.

Their point of view is ... if you are not with them then you are against them. Therefore they do not want to cooperate and associate with anyone. In natural and real shakti pat nobody enters into you, and neither do you enter into somebody else, but it is the blossoming of the individual consciousness into the Cosmic Consciousness.

No doubt the seekers apparently may feel the entry of some entity into them, but it is just contrary to the fact. On proper examination they can analyze truth and can dismiss these pseudo-phenomena as taken for granted. For example, if we go by train from New York City to Washington, we express our thoughts that Washington is coming, but this expression is taken for granted. On careful analysis we find that it is not Washington that is coming, but we are coming. Likewise seekers apparently may feel entry of some entity or some person or teacher into them, but on final analysis they will find it is nothing but a projection of their own unconscious and subconscious mind. Guru is only one – there are not many gurus. And that guru is God. Other gurus are and should be respected in the light of God alone, not as a separate entity.

Shakti Pat and Kundalini

कुण्डलिन्यां समुद्धता गायत्री प्राणधारिणी ।
प्राणविद्या महाविद्या यस्तां वेत्ति स वेदवित् ॥

**KUNDALINYAM SAMUDBHUTA
GAYATRI PRANADHARINI PRANAVIDYA
MAHAVIDYA YASTAM VETTI SA VEDAVIT.**

Awakening of the divine power, kundalini,
and shakti pat are synonymous.
Kundalini is always awakened, but is not
experienced. The experience of this dormant
cosmic energy is called shakti pat.

As long as this kundalini force remains
dormant and asleep, so long man remains
isolated from the rest of the universe; he
remains in the state of ignorance which is the
cause of helplessness, hopelessness,
frustration, depression, anxieties, worries,
lack of self-security and self-confidence
consequently ending in jealousy, hatred, fear,
phobia, various physical and mental
sufferings, and finally in suicidal tendency.
The awakening of Kundalini brings the five
following important factors into human
experience:

1. Experience of the state of vibration, in
and out; this includes all systems of the body
especially respiratory system, heart and
circulation, and electrical waves including the
nervous system.

2. The role of liquid energy; this includes blood, plasma, hormones, enzymes, chemical, bio-chemical and biological forces.

3. Manifestation of light and color with various types of extrasensory perceptions, and other various supernatural phenomena.

4. Opening of the chakras from muladhara up to sahasrara. As the kundalini rises from muladhara to sahasrara through susumna it pierces an infinite number of chakras.

Grossly all these chakras are grouped into seven chakras, like seven days and seven colors.

5. Union of creative energy with cognitive energy. As kundalini pierces the chakras, so new levels of consciousness are opened finally this current becomes absolutely cosmic in nature and man experiences in that state, union with the supreme self.

In philosophical and religious language this union is called by various names, such as the union of RADHA and KRISHNA. The Sanskrit word is 'DHARA' which means ... 'current of kundalini operating in the relative world'. But when this current begins to rise up it becomes 'RADHA' and the supreme force which attracts it up is called 'KRISHNA'.

Thus the meaning of RADHA-KRISHNA in the sense of kundalini awakening is the meeting of supreme cosmic creative energy with the supreme consciousness. This current is also called 'GANGA' because with the relative universe turns back into the heavenly state. It is also called 'SHIVA-SHAKTI-SAMMELANAM' that is to say the meeting of the shakti or primordial energy with Shiva, supreme consciousness.

How shakti is awakened

There are innumerable ways, but the following are the most prominent of them:

Bhakti Yoga   Mantra Yoga
Jnana Yoga   Hatha Yoga
Karma Yoga   Pranayama
Asanas   Charity,

Unselfish service to mankind, previous incarnations, good karma, various bandhas (locks) and mudras. In short, anything which involves the friction of energy and consciousness, matter and mind, mind and spirit, individual soul and supreme soul, is transformed into kindling of the sleeping fire of cognition.

The primal energy rising through the central nervous system piercing all chakras involves the evolution and involution of the entire universe, subjective as well as objective with its past, present and future phenomena.

The heart is the center of unity and the seat of the manifestation of the supreme self. The brain is the machine like cosmic computer through which mind multiplies the center of unity into various phenomena. Thus the mystery of the universe begins to reveal its true operation, and the sadhaka begins to experience multiplicity in the unity and unity as the foundation of multiplicity. In other words, he experiences the presence of his Self in all beings and all beings in his own Self.

Manifestations are divided into three classes:

Physically, a person during awakening of kundalini shakti can experience an automatic and spontaneous flow of energy during hatha yoga exercises. In short, hatha yoga becomes natural, spontaneous and automatic. Ones body becomes light and ones voice becomes very sweet.

Psychologically, he experiences tingling sensations of numbness, heat and cold, including various visions and supernatural manifestations.

Spiritually, he feels himself in the state of progressive bliss, tranquility and cosmic unity.

Again, all these manifestations are divided into two forms, natural and pathological:

Natural movement includes the natural awakening of kundalini. He who is passing through natural and mental illness, and he experiences bliss without interference or interruption.

Pathological awakening always triggers psychosomatic manifestations, and it presents management problems. Such a person needs proper guidance and help, medically and spiritually.

Case Histories

It is already stated that shakti pat triggered with schizophrenia becomes a complicated problem. Here are some cases whose histories will give to the reader a proper way to understand the psychological problems involved in it, and to understand the exact nature of kundalini arising. Thus a Sadhaka can protect himself from the consequences and side effects leading to schizophrenia.

Case 1

Mr. A., a medical officer (M.D.) from San Francisco, once experienced something like the opening of a screw at the base of his spine and the rising of electrical charges up to the crown of his head. He was shocked and surprised, and he felt something like his soul passing out of his body, piercing the roof of his apartment, and he experienced shining stars in the day light. This experience lasted about six hours, and ultimately he experienced his soul returning back into his physical body.

Since he was shocked and surprised, he became fearful and began to think of it as something like a psychiatric manifestation.

After a gap of many years of this manifestation he consulted me, and after getting proper understanding he became absolutely free from all fears, and now he is very blissful and teaches kundalini yoga and shakti pat.

Case 2

Mr. B., an Italian born gentleman living in the USA, once felt the opening of the screw at the base of the spine, and rising of electrical waves toward the crown of the head, shaking, jerking of the body, chattering of the teeth, seizures like epileptic fits, tremendous manifestations of heat and cold from base of spine up to the head, which made him extremely fearful. He had psychiatric consultation and was taking nearly fifteen pills of thorazine a day to calm himself down from the tremendous agitation.

Psychiatric treatment included frequent electric shocks and various other treatments including psychotherapy. Thus he passed ten years under psychotherapy with no results. Anyhow, he came to know me and consulted me about this matter. After introducing him to Kundalini Yoga he was given many books to read, yoga relaxation and meditation along with HathaYoga postures were properly introduced to him, and after two months treatment he became an absolutely extraordinary man with the feeling of

blessedness. Now he is extremely grateful to
the books written on Kundalini Yoga and to
the practice of yoga meditation.

Case 3

Miss C., a divorced young lady, extremely
beautiful, felt continuously and constantly
opening of the screw at the base of the spine
and surge of electrical charges toward the
crown of the head with intolerable heat and
cold and shaking of the body. Due to this she
was divorced - her husband became afraid of
her. She received many years of psychiatric
service with no result. Once she came to
Ananda Ashram to consult me, and after
knowing this manifestation as the awakening
of Kundalini, her panic and fear disappeared.
Still she feels in the same way, but now she
enjoys these manifestations blissfully. All her
fearful manifestations are transformed now
into divine manifestations and blissful moods.
She is supremely happy and blissful and
thankful to these manifestations.

Case 4

Mr. D. from Germany felt tremendous force
of electrical charges in the center of his
abdomen and began to experience something
like a whirlpool of electrical charges moving
up and down, practically becoming out of

order. He was hearing a tremendous noise in his head -he was in hospital for six months with no results. One day he attended my lecture in Germany and requested a consultation. After being given yoga exercises, the proper way of meditation and relaxation and after reading some books on this topic he became absolutely free from all fear and phobia. Now he enjoys these manifestations, and he also saved his wife who was passing through the same type of manifestations.

Case 5

Mr. E. began to feel sudden tremendous jerks with the sensation of tremendous heat and cold and numbness all over the body. Later on these jerks were increased in the form of fits. He became absolutely confused and terrified. Sometimes he was howling like a donkey and barking like a dog. Because of this intolerable manifestation he was admitted into Dhana Mental Institute in Bombay. Remaining there one year with no results he was discharged, and he consulted Kundalini Yoga teachers, and they advised him to see me. After checking his diet, correcting his routine practice, giving him yoga exercises, meditation, and several books to read on the topic, he became absolutely free from pathological symptoms. Now he is very blissful and thankful to all these manifestations.

Case 6

Miss F. from USA experienced tremendous jerks all over the body, and began to experience opening of the screw in the center of her abdomen and electrical charges all over the body, tremendous yawning and loss of appetite. This condition lasted about five years. She consulted me in San Francisco, and after two months of proper Kundalini Yoga exercises she became perfectly super-normal and her appetite returned. She is now studying Indian philosophy and preparing extensive literature on Kundalini Yoga.

Case 7

Mrs. G., PH. D. in psychology, gradually and progressively developed tremendous and uncontrollable howling sounds - sometimes it was like thundering and roaring, sometimes growling. These sounds became progressively so intolerable that they created serious concern in the mind of her family members regarding her physical and mental health. Sometimes her sounds would produce tremendous jerks in the people sitting around her.

She consulted me and also Shri Baba Muktanandaji and after proper introduction of Kundalini Yoga she became absolutely happy and divinely blissful. Still she has these roaring sounds, but they are gradually changing into rumbling and rhythmical vibration. Her fear having disappeared for good. She is now teaching Kundalini Yoga, meditation and psychology.

Case 8

Miss H. from the Polynesian Islands was manifesting tremendously bizarre behavior and extraordinary unusual jerks and electrical charges all over the body. Sometimes these jerks were so powerful that they created the fear of death. She joined the Yoga Society of San Francisco and was advised to see Shri Baba Muktananda Maharaj also. New she is very happy, fearless, and began to enjoy the blissful rising of Kundalini.

Case 9

Miss I. was attending yoga programs, and all of a sudden she experienced electrical jerks in her body, and these jerks were transformed finally into a rhythmic dance. She had already some introduction of Kundalini Yoga, therefore she was not panicky and fearful, but was doubtful whether the manifestations were truly related to Shakti Pat, or to some psychopathological condition. After checking her diet, postures and meditation, she was transformed into divine bliss. Later on she did tremendous study of Kundalini Yoga and finally she became a teacher of Kundalini Yoga and Shakti Pat.

Case 10

Mr. J., a young boy from Virginia, attended my lecture in the Buddhist Academy in 1958. He experienced an electrical shock and became unconscious all of a sudden. In spite of this difficulty I completed my meditation program peacefully and I brought this boy with the help of some friends into the hospital in Welfare Island, where I was working at that time. After six hours he became conscious with divine bliss and unusual experience. "I never experienced such a tremendous ocean of light and color, peace, and bliss", he said. He then began to speak Sanskrit which he did not know before. Later on he practiced yoga meditation, relaxation and the study of Sanskrit. Thus he continued to work with me for five years. After that he was drafted into the military service and I regularly receive his letters of gratefulness and thankfulness. He is extremely happy in his study and practice of meditation.

Note

During my psychiatric consultations and yogic consultations I received a tremendous number of friends with partial or complete manifestations of shakti pat, but they were confused and mingled with psychopathological and psychiatric manifestations. After conquering their psychopathological conditions, checking their psychopathological conditions, checking their diets and daily activities of life with proper meditation, practically all became free from all dangerous consequences, and on the contrary they now enjoy perfect divine bliss.

Only ten cases are quoted here for the sake of the readers. If I were to write every case I would have a book. I'm sure and I hope readers will enjoy this preliminary introduction to shakti pat and kundalini rising. All of Gopi Krishna's books are highly recommended. The personal history of Chaitanya Mahaprabhu written by Das Gupta is also highly recommended to readers.

There is tremendous literature on this topic in the Sanskrit language for which one can consult books on Tantra Yoga and Kundalini Yoga, which describe the rising of the Kundalini and Shakti Pat in detail.

I hope this article will help those who are passing through the manifestation of Shakti Pat, especially those who have some psychopathological and psychosomatic difficulties. For further detail they can consult any teacher expert on this topic.

Other Titles in this Series
BY PILGRIMS PUBLISHING

For Catalog & More Information, Write To:
PILGRIMS BOOK HOUSE
P.O Box: 3872, Thamel
Kathmandu, Nepal
Tel: 977-1- 424942, 425919
Fax: 977-1- 424943
Email: pilgrims@wlink.com.np
Website: www.pilgrimsbooks.com